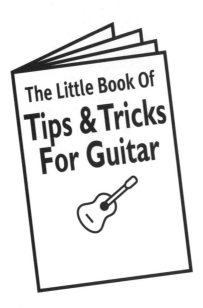

The Little Book Of
Tips & Tricks
For Guitar

Wise Publications
London/New York/Sydney/Paris/Copenhagen/Madrid

Exclusive distributors:
Music Sales Limited
8/9 Frith Street, London W1V 5TZ, England.
Music Sales Corporation
257 Park Avenue South, New York, NY10010,
United States of America.
Music Sales Pty Limited
120 Rothschild Avenue
Rosebery, NSW 2018, Australia.

Order No.AM954767
ISBN 0-7119-7821-2
This book © Copyright 1999 by Wise Publications

Written by Rikky Rooksby
Book engraved by Digital Music Art
Photographs by courtesy of George Taylor

Cover design by Trickett & Webb

Printed in Great Britain by
Printwise (Haverhill) Limited, Suffolk.

Guitar Tablature Explained

THE MUSICAL STAVE shows pitches and rhythms and is divided by lines into bars. Pitches are named after the first seven letters of the alphabet.

TABLATURE graphically represents the guitar fingerboard. Each horizontal line represents a string, and each number represents a fret.

4th string, 2nd fret   1st & 2nd strings open, played together   open D chord

definitions for special guitar notation

SEMI-TONE BEND: Strike the note and bend up a semi-tone (1/2 step).

WHOLE-TONE BEND: Strike the note and bend up a whole-tone (whole step).

GRACE NOTE BEND: Strike the note and bend as indicated. Play the first note as quickly as possible.

QUARTER-TONE BEND: Strike the note and bend up a 1/4 step.

HAMMER-ON: Strike the first (lower) note with one finger, then sound the higher note (on the same string) with another finger by fretting it without picking.

PULL-OFF: Place both fingers on the notes to be sounded. Strike the first note and without picking, pull the finger off to sound the second (lower) note.

BEND & RELEASE: Strike the note and bend up as indicated, then release back to the original note.

LEGATO SLIDE (GLISS): Strike the first note and then slide the same fret-hand finger up or down to the second note. The second note is not struck.

SHIFT SLIDE (GLISS & RESTRIKE): Same as legato slide, except the second note is struck.

Contents

Technique Tips

Gear

Tricks for Soloists

Rhythm Tips

Style Ideas

Check Your Hand Positions

Playing the guitar is much easier when you use good right and left hand positioning.

The Thumb

Place your left hand (the fretting hand) on the fretboard. Make sure that your thumb remains vertical and roughly somewhere behind the first finger and second finger.

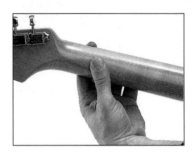

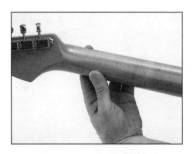

Bad Technique!

Never let the palm of this hand touch the neck in order to exert pressure - such a position will completely ruin the movement of the fingers. Allow the thumb to retain its natural curve.

Barre Chords

When attempting a barre chord, lower the thumb so that its end is lower than the top of the finger-board.

String Bending

When bending strings curl the thumb slightly over the top of the neck to get more leverage. Usually it is perfectly okay to have half an inch of the thumb showing.

Strumming

When strumming the main movement comes from the arm rather than the hand, although the hand can make small accentuating movements. There's no need to sweep too far below the strings or rise too far above them.

Picking Technique

The action for picking notes is very different: the movement is from the hand, primarily the thumb and first finger (holding the pick). The forearm does not move back and forth. You may find it easier to put the forearm down onto the body of the guitar to stabilise the hand.

Guide Fingers (1)

One useful thing to be aware of in fingering is the *guide finger*. This is a finger that moves up or down a string during a sequence of changes providing continuity making the changes easier.

In this first example you'll find a sequence of sixths (notes an interval of a sixth apart), which are often used as decorative lead figures in guitar playing. Notice that the second finger acts as a guide, always on the lowest note of each pair, whereas the upper note is played either with the first or third finger.

In the second example there is a sequence of thirds. In bars 1-2 the second finger acts as a guide, and in bars 3-4, it's the first finger.

Guide Fingers (2)

When playing a chord progression always check if there is a finger that doesn't need to move, or a finger that only needs to move up or down a string.

Try the following chord sequence:

| C | ╱ | A m | ╱ | | D m^7 | ╱ | ╱ | B^7 | | E add^9 | ╱ | C♯m^7 | ╱ | |

| C♯^{7}sus^4 | ╱ | B sus^4 | ╱ | | A^{13} | E^9 | ▬ | | |

Notice how the first finger doesn't move until B7; how the third finger stays still as you go from Dm7 to B7; how the fourth finger stays still going to Eadd9; how the third finger is a guide up the 4th string as you change to C#m7 and so on.

Each chord is connected to the next either by a finger that doesn't move or one that moves up or down a string.

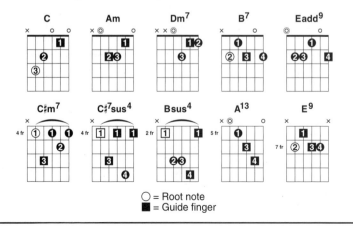

○ = Root note
■ = Guide finger

How To Use A Capo (1) - Transposing The Easy Way

The capodastro - 'capo' for short - is a very useful piece of equipment for guitarists. Imagine you had to play the following chord progression:

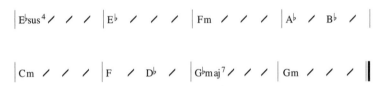

Every one of these chords is a barre chord. Such a progression can become very tiring for the fretting hand and inhibits the decoration of the sequence because almost every chord requires that all the fingers be used. A capo solves the problem neatly.

By placing a capo at the first fret all the chords can be played with the shape of the chord one semitone lower. Most of these now become a lot easier to play. The chord in brackets is the actual pitch; the chord name is the familiar open position shape.

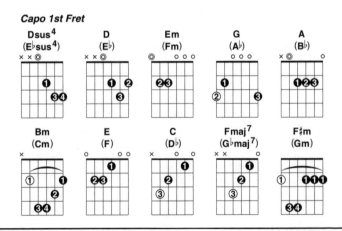

10

How To Use A Capo (2) - Instant Chord Changes

Here's another example.
Look at the chord sequence below:

A capo

| C♯ / / / | C♯maj⁷ / / / | C♯⁷ / / / | D♯m / F♯ / |

| G♯⁷ / / / | A♯m¹¹ / / / | D♯⁷ / / / | E♯m / B / ‖ |

Without a capo this would be very tiring for the fretting hand. With a capo at the fourth fret it becomes much easier.

The chord boxes give the shape name first (as if open position) and the actual pitch second. The capo is at the fourth fret, four frets is two tones, therefore each chord is represented by the shape two tones below it.

Capo 4th Fret

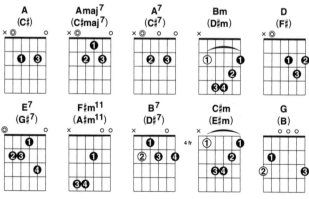

11

How To Use A Capo (3) - Better Fingerpicking

A capo can be used to produce different tones from the guitar. If the capo is placed quite high on the neck the sound changes, becoming higher and brighter.

Another consequence of a high capo is that it becomes possible to finger combinations of notes which would be impossible lower down. This arises because the frets are closer together.

This short finger-picked piece has many note clusters which are only playable because the capo is at the seventh fret. Listen out for the chiming effect caused by notes that are either very close (as in bars 2 and 7) or at the same pitch (bar 3).

Note that the TAB numbers refer to the capoed guitar, so that the first note is two frets above the capo, which is actually the 9th fret of the guitar.

How To Use A Capo (4) - Create A Fuller Sound

Another great use of a capo is to achieve a fuller sound in a guitar duo. Imagine you're playing a song with this chord progression:

The first five chord boxes show how one guitar could play this sequence with the usual chord shapes.

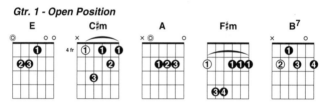

The second five chord boxes show the same chords played on another guitar with a capo at the seventh position. The shape name comes first, the actual pitch in brackets.

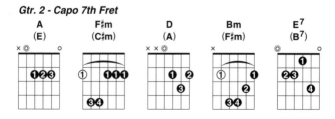

When both guitars are playing the sound is fuller because guitar 2's chords are pitched higher, creating a 12-string effect.

Make It Easy On Yourself - The Art Of Fingering

Some of the techniques you will use to improve your playing will be visible (eg. string-bending or damping) and some will be invisible - i.e. it's not immediately obvious that you're doing anything.

One such invisible technique is fingering - the art of knowing which fingers should hold down notes and chords. If you get your fingering right, things will be easier to play.

Sometimes it's a good idea to change the fingering of a common chord in order to make a change easier. Check out these five examples to find out how altering the fingering can make certain chord changes easier.

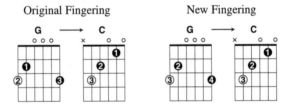

Refingering this G chord makes it easier to change to C because your 2nd and 3rd fingers only need to move across one string from the bottom two strings.

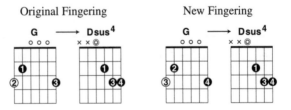

By refingering this G chord, your 4th finger can remain in place as you change to Dsus4.

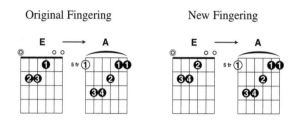

Here, by changing the 1st, 2nd and 3rd fingers in the E chord to 2nd, 3rd and 4th, it becomes easier to move up one fret and add a first finger barre, to form the A chord.

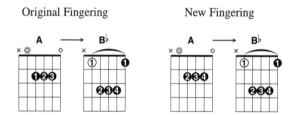

Changing to barre chords can be made much easier by altering the fingering slightly - now all you have to do is move the shape to its new position and add the barre.

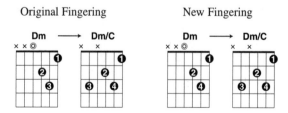

This change in bass note can be simplified by refingering the Dm chord to leave your 3rd finger free to play the C on the D string.

Pick & Fingers

One of the most useful picking hand techniques is the ability to use a pick and fingers together. For this reason the pick should always be held between the thumb and the first finger and not the second finger.

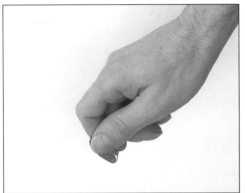

Pick Grip

Grip the pick firmly with the flat part of the thumb, against the side of the first finger.

Pick and Fingers

Here, the pick is being held in the normal way, but the other fingers are also being used to pick the strings. This enables you to play more strings at once.

The next example gives you an opportunity to try this approach. The pick always hits the lowest note with a down stroke, the second and third fingers pluck the other notes. Once you get the hang of it, gradually speed up. Eventually you'll hear an almost classical effect.

p m a p m a p m a p m a (etc.)

The pick and fingers technique offers a finger-picking effect but leaves you with the option of moving into single-note lead soloing or heavy strumming.

It's the best of both worlds!

The example above is labelled with the fingers to use for finger-picking. P refers to the pick, which should be held in the usual way, while using the M and A fingers to pluck the other strings.

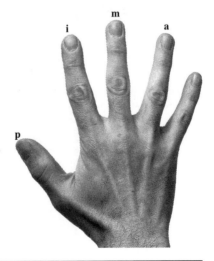

17

More Tones From Your Electric Guitar

Electric guitarists tend to associate the number of pickups / pick-up selection they have with the number of tones they can get from their instrument. Actually, you can always get more tones from your guitar without buying any more equipment.

Pickup Selection

Select any pickup on your guitar and make sure you have a clean sound and enough volume to hear clearly.

Volume control

Pickup

Tone controls

Your Usual Tone

Strike the G string wherever your picking hand normally hits it. That establishes your usual tone.

Changing the tone

Now strike the string over the very end of the fingerboard. It's a different tone even though you're on the same pickup.

Keep striking the G string but gradually move from over the fingerboard toward the bridge.

Experiment!

As you do this you will hear the tone changing continually and becoming thinner, more brittle and more trebly as you approach the bridge.

Change pickups and repeat the process. You will hear different tones. You can use these tones in your playing simply by moving your picking hand a few inches.

Don't forget that the volume and tone pots on your guitar will also have an effect on tone. For a jazzy underwater sound, try the neck pickup with the tone wound off.

Violin Tone

There's one great sound-effect you can get from an electric guitar at no extra expense: violin-tone. To do it you need a fair amount of volume from the amplifier.

Begin by turning the volume off on the guitar itself. Then curl your little finger around the volume pot. Strike the string and turn the volume up with your finger. If you do it correctly the note you have struck will increase in volume. Guitar notes usually decay from loud to soft. If the timing is good you won't hear the actual strike of the string, the percussive effect which is typical of a guitar being played with a pick (or fingers). The string should already be vibrating when the volume is still off. As you turn the pot a note will appear which seems not to have been struck.

Turning the pot and striking strings at the same time can be tricky, and a lot depends on the layout of your guitar and how far the volume pots are from the strings. If you're using a distorted sound try hammering-on the notes with your fretting hand - that saves having to actually strike the strings.

Violin-tone also sounds great with echo. You can buy a volume pedal which allows you to create the effect with your foot.

Violining

This technique is easier on a *Strat* than a *Les Paul* due to the position of the volume control.

Listen to *Xanadu* by Rush, and *Cathedral* by Eddie Van Halen for classic examples of this technique.

Wah-Wah

Wah-wah pedals were first used in the late 1960s and remain a popular effect with electric guitarists.

Different pedals have a different action - the width of the angle through which the pedal travels from open to shut positions. When the pedal is open the treble frequencies are cut giving a muted sound. When the pedal is shut the treble frequencies are boosted. You can set the pedal to either of these positions and simply leave it there.

For the wah sound itself there is a critical angle (usually about half-way down) at which the audible change in the note is at its maximum. To play a wah-wah successfully you need to 'ride' that point the way a surfer rides a wave. You don't need to pump the pedal up and down. Just a subtle touch back and forth on that 'cross-over' point will do the trick.

To get the classic 'Shaft' soundtrack sound, mute all the strings and strum 16ths (four times each beat) slowly moving the pedal up and down. Another classic effect is to play a lead phrase with a few repeated notes and gradually move the pedal from open to shut and back again. The changing frequencies will be more noticeable because the notes are remaining the same.

Wah-Wah

The much loved 'cry-baby' wah-wah pedal - never leave the house without one!

Maximum Overdrive - Using a Power Soak

The trouble with big valve amps is that by the time you've turned them up far enough to get a rich distortion from the valves the volume level is unmanageable and everyone else in the band (or your neighbours) are complaining.

There is a gadget which will help you with this. It's a circuit that acts as an attenuator, absorbing (or 'soaking') some of the amp's power before it reaches the speakers. It plugs in between the amp head and the speaker cabinet and usually has several settings depending on how much energy you want to absorb. Instant valve distortion with no artificial ingredients and you get to keep two functioning ear-drums!

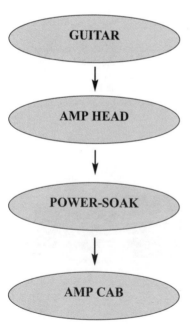

Once you have your amp set up with the power soak as shown here, you will find that you can alter the sound of your guitar quite drastically, simply by altering the volume control on the guitar. Turn the volume right down for a punchy, clean sound ideal for rhythm playing, or turn it right up for a screaming, distorted solo.

You'll also find that this set-up will make your guitar much more responsive to subtleties of touch and articulation - the playing of Jimi Hendrix being a classic example.

Using Two Distortion Circuits

Rock players often find that they need not one but two distortion sounds - one for rhythm and the other for lead. The problem with trying to use one distortion sound is that if it is thick enough for single note lead playing it makes chords sound mushy, and if it is clear enough for the chords it doesn't have enough sustain and penetration for lead.

One way out of this is to use the volume pot on the guitar. Turn this full on. Now adjust your distortion circuit (in a pedal or in the amp) until you get the type of distortion you want for lead, and that you have the volume level you need for the solo. Now turn the volume pot down until you find a level that's right for rhythm. Some of the distortion will thin out because the pickup isn't being driven flat-out.

Another technique is to have two distortion / overdrive circuits running. Make sure the volume on your guitar is pretty much up full. Then set the first distortion to give you a good rhythm sound. Now set the second to add a little extra distortion and more volume by turning up its own volume control. Then when you want to solo you can just turn on the second distortion circuit. The first circuit could be in the amp itself; the second could be a pedal. Pedals labelled as 'overdrive' rather than out-and-out distortions are sufficient for this purpose.

More Gadgets...

Here are two common effects pedals you could use to achieve the above effect - a Boss OD-1 Overdrive and an Ibanez Tube Screamer.

How To Play Lead

So, you'd like to start playing solos, but don't know how to go about it? Here's a quick way to get you started...

These three scales represent A pentatonic minor. This has five notes: A C D E G. The first scale is situated at the 5th fret. The second is basically the same except there is a little extension at the top, which takes you a few frets higher. The third scale is one octave higher than the first. These patterns cover quite a bit of the fretboard and provide ample material for a solo.

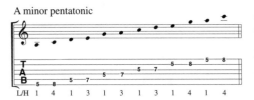

A Pentatonic Minor

This is the basic moveable pattern, and doesn't use finger extensions or changes of hand position.

...with extension

You'll find yourself playing some different phrases with this pattern, which shifts position to get right up to the 12th fret.

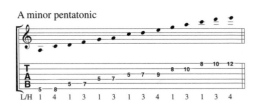

An Octave Higher

Don't be put off by the high numbers, the frets are closer together at the top of neck so there's less stress on your fingers.

Try using these scales over a 12-bar sequence in A or A minor. And here's the magic bit: you can also use them for anything in the key of C major. Why? Because every pentatonic minor scale is also the pentatonic major of the note three semitones higher (A to C = 3 semitones). It is the chord sequence that will decide whether the scale is heard as A pentatonic minor or C pentatonic major.

Lead With Open Strings

Playing single note lead runs can sometimes sound a bit thin, especially in a three-piece band. Here's a way of making a bigger sound as you solo - by using an open string.

If you're playing in a key where E, B or G is an important note (i.e. the root or the 5th of the scale), major or minor, you can play lead phrases up and down an adjacent string whilst hitting the open string at the same time.

The example shows an ascending lead melody in E major with an open string E sounding above it all the way through. Just add a touch of distortion and echo for a big sound.

String Clearance

Make sure you lift up onto the tips of your fingers to ensure the top E (1st) string rings out clearly while you fret notes on the B (2nd) string.

Riff With Open Strings

Open strings can also be used to make a riff sound bigger. When they occur as bass notes below a moving line they're called 'pedal notes'. On the guitar, E A and D are possible pedal notes.

In this example a riff / melody is moving up and down the G string on a scale known as the Dorian mode (D E F G A B C D). Underneath, the D string is sounding throughout. The effect is surprisingly full. Again, effects such as distortion, chorus and/or echo will make it fuller.

The Dorian Mode

Much used by Carlos Santana, this mode is basically a natural minor with a sharpened 6th.

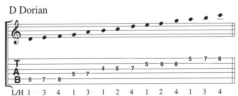

D Dorian

Fingering A Lead Run

It's not just chord sequences that benefit from good fingering. Obviously, fingering becomes crucial if you're trying to play at speed.

One good approach to fingering single note runs is to organise everything into a four-fret 'box' in which each finger is allocated to one fret. With these positions, playing fast lead runs becomes a lot easier. The Roman numeral over the stave indicates which position (or fret) you should start at.

The example below starts at second position, with each finger looking after one fret. In bars 5-6 the solo changes position several times - but watch what happens to the fingering. Bar 7 extends the 'box' to five frets because further up the neck, the frets are sufficiently close together enough to allow the fingers to cover five frets.

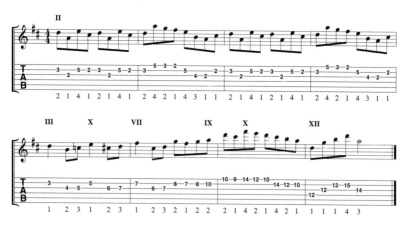

Remember that if a lead run involves bending notes a different fingering will have to be adopted to avoid bending with the weak little finger.

Play Lead Without Learning Scales!

You might think that in order to play lead solos you have to know lots of scales. Here's a trick that will allow you to create some great solos by using phrases based on chords rather than scales.

In this example the first four bars use triad figures (a triad is any chord consisting of three notes). In bars 5-8 these are repeated and extended downwards. Notice how these figures can incorporate bends and pull-offs.

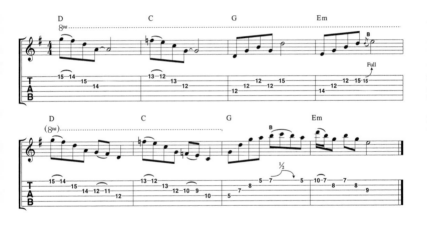

Because you're outlining the chords themselves, and following the chord changes, your playing will sound more melodic. This is a very different concept to the standard approach, where you use one scale that will work over an entire chord sequence.

This is the beginning of what jazz musicians would call "playing over the changes", where the soloist adopts a different set of scales and arpeggios for every chord change, and is also an approach that can be used effectively in nearly all forms of music.

Getting The Most From A Lead Lick

Here's another useful trick for playing lead licks without learning hundreds of phrases. Sometimes all you need to do is make different use of a phrase you already know.

Remember this important rule: the musical value of a lead phrase or note depends upon the harmony that supports it. The practical effect of this is that playing the same phrase over different chords will alter its sound.

Try this two bar phrase over a C chord. Under the stave/TAB notation you'll find an analysis of its harmonic value - in other words, what the notes mean in terms of the supporting C chord. The numbers that are circled - 1, 3, 5 - are the notes of C major. The more circled numbers, the better the lick will sound.

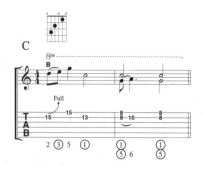

The following five diagrams are an analysis of the same notes played against the other chords in the key of C major: Dm, Em, F, G, and Am. The notes stay the same but their harmonic value (indicated by the numbers) has changed and consequently the sound changes.

This is true of any lead phrase or note repeated over a changing set of chords.

Professional Solos - With No Effort!

Check out the following chord progression:

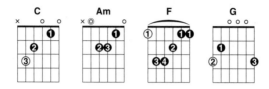

This is in the key of C major. Most guitarists would automatically use a C major pentatonic or A minor pentatonic scale to solo over this.

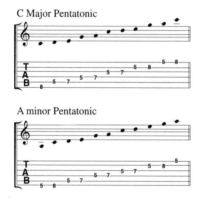

Instead, try playing E minor pentatonic. Here's the scale, along with a few bars of lead solo.

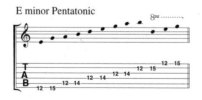

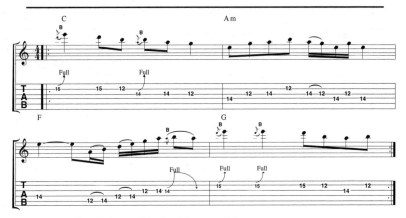

How is it possible for this to work?

The full C major scale is:	C D E F G A B C
C major pentatonic is:	C D E G A
E minor pentatonic is:	E G A B D

You can see from this that none of the notes from C pentatonic and E pentatonic minor fall outside those found in the full C major scale, and therefore they won't clash. However, these two scales do differ slightly. The diagram below shows the notes common to both scales (arrowed) and the notes which differ (B & C, circled).

In E minor pentatonic the key note is missing (C), which gives the scale an unusual quality, especially if you play the entire solo using it rather than combining it with a C scale. To do this in other major keys simply use the pentatonic minor which is two tones above your key note.

Play Blues Lead - The Easy Way

Most inexperienced blues players have a tendency to over-use the pentatonic minor. Here's a brilliant and very easy trick for instantly transforming the sound of your blues solos.

You should recognise the first two scales: A pentatonic minor followed by an 'extension' box around the 8th fret which goes on top of it.

The extension box is the upper part of the next position of the A pentatonic minor, and many players find this fragment of it invaluable for extending the range of the basic scale.

A Pentatonic Minor

This is the first blues scale many people learn, but it's a lot more versatile than you might realise.

Extension Box

Try this useful extension to the A pentatonic minor for a little more range and a lot more options.

Imagine you're playing a 12-bar in A. If you move these scale patterns down three frets they automatically convert into the major pentatonic for the same key - so you don't have to learn a new pattern!

This works anywhere on the neck above the first couple of frets. Moving down three frets creates a radical change in tone. The pentatonic major sounds much more upbeat.

Mixing the two scales will make your blues solos more interesting.

A Pentatonic Major

Make sure you know this easy 'rule' so you can use this as a substitute for the pentatonic minor.

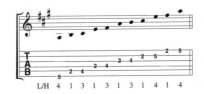

Extension Box

The same rule will apply to this A pentatonic minor extension box.

Remember, this only works in a major key. In other words, in a major key you can play pentatonic minor and major scales. In a minor key you can't play any major scales - believe me, they won't sound good!

Dropped D Tuning For Rockers

One area of guitar-playing which has become increasingly popular is the use of altered and open tunings. These put new sounds within the reach of the guitarist and can stimulate creativity.

One popular tuning which is easy to use is 'dropped D'. For this, just tune the bottom E down a tone to D. You can check if it's in tune either by comparing it with the open fourth string (which is a D one octave higher) or by holding down the 7th fret on the bottom string and checking that it is the same as the open A.

Heavy rock / grunge players like this tuning because it creates a low, easily fingered 'power-chord'. It also enables you to play that classic rock'n'roll rhythm figure featured elsewhere in this book with much less of a stretch.

Tuning Guide						
String number	6	5	4	3	2	1
Standard tuning	E	A	D	G	B	E
This tuning	**D**	**A**	**D**	**G**	**B**	**E**
Alteration necessary	-2	-	-	-	-	-
Interval between strings (in semitones/frets)	7	5	5	4	5	

Have a go at this example - remember, you can now play the bottom strings on the D chord.

Dropped D Tuning For Finger Pickers

Dropped D tuning is also popular with finger-pickers. In folk styles, the tuning offers an octave of two open string Ds (the sixth and fourth strings) which can be played by the thumb in an alternating movement in the bass.

As these notes are open strings the fretting hand is free to go where it wishes and play a melody.

Try the following piece to get a taste for this folk bass and melody style.

Tuning Guide						
String number	6	5	4	3	2	1
Standard tuning	E	A	D	G	B	E
This tuning	**D**	**A**	**D**	**G**	**B**	**E**
Alteration necessary	-2	-	-	-	-	-
Interval between strings (in semitones/frets)	7	5	5	4	5	

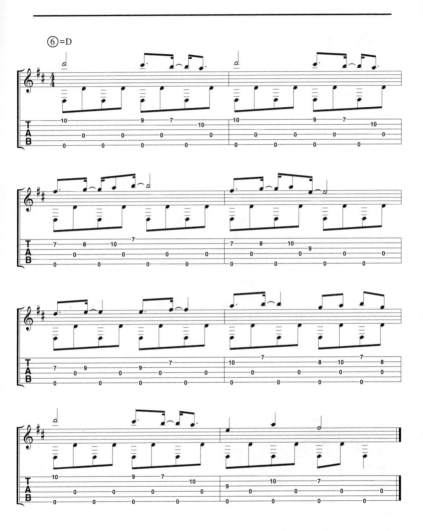

Going Up With D

It's fun to experiment with chord shapes on the guitar. All you need to do is pick a shape, move it up the neck, and find out where it sounds good.

The D chord is a good shape to do this with. The eight chord boxes below show you how your fingers hold down a series of major triads while the D note sounds underneath.

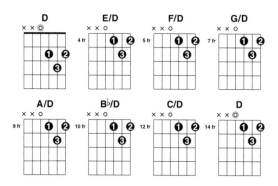

D Major shape

Slash chords, such as the F/D chord shown above, can often be named in a number of ways. F/D literally means an F chord with a D note in the bass, but it could also be called Dm7, as it contains the notes D, F, A and C, which are the 1st, 3rd, 5th and 7th notes of the D minor scale.

Going Up With C

Here's another example of moving up a chord shape to see what happens. Start with an ordinary C chord. Note that it has three fretted notes (C, E and C) and two open strings (G and E). As the shape moves up the neck the fretted notes always maintain the same relation to each other, but the open strings remain G and E. These open notes form new relationships with each shape, fret by fret.

In the chord boxes you'll notice that sometimes there's a finger on the top string - this is to make the shapes more effective.

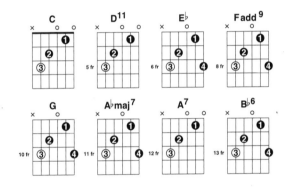

C Major shape

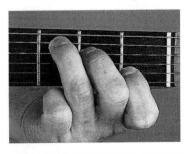

41

How To Play Slide Guitar in Standard Tuning

Slide or bottleneck guitar is often associated with open tunings such as G (D G D G B D) or A (E A E A C♯ E). However, what happens if you need to play some bottleneck chords in standard tuning? Here's a tip.

To get a major or minor chord you only need three notes. This is called a triad. The top three strings make a minor triad (EBG) - E minor in fact with the root note at the top. The second, third and fourth strings (BGD) make a major triad - G major, with the root note in the middle.

By using the right fret positions and combination of strings you can play these major and minor triads along with any chord progression in any key. The chord boxes below show the 7 most likely chords for a song in C major.

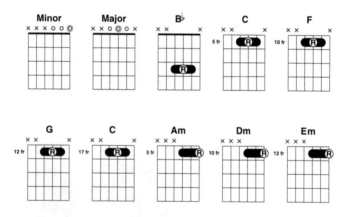

The 'R' in each slide guitar chord simply shows you where the root note of the chord can be found.

Power-chords

To get a heavier, tougher guitar sound when playing a chord sequence, try using 'power-chords'. The correct term for these is 'fifths'. They're written C5, F5, G5, etc.

The first five chord boxes show some fifths with just two notes - these can sound very distorted. Fifth chords are neither major nor minor. That means you can play them underneath a chord progression regardless of whether it is in a major key (C, F, G) or a minor one (Cm, Fm, Gm).

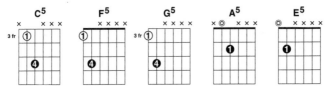

The second five chord boxes allow you to bring in a few more strings. Notice that in each case you haven't added any different notes - it's still only two in each case - they're just being doubled or trebled.

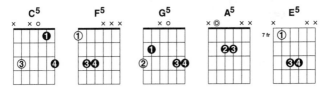

Barre Alternative

You can play the upper notes of the moveable power-chords (such as E5 and F5 in the second chord group above) with a third or even fourth finger partial barre, just lay a finger flat across both strings.

More Power-Chords

The golden rule about chords on the guitar is this: the more complicated they are the fewer places in which you'll be able to play them.

As there are only two notes in a power-chord, they can be found in many different positions all over the fretboard.

The chordboxes below show 10 different ways of playing an A5.

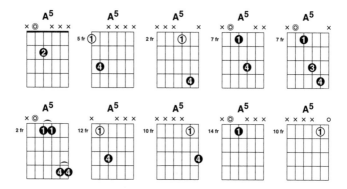

The same applies to all other power-chords, but especially those that include open strings. Try to find as many E5 and D5 shapes as you can, all over the fretboard. Here are a few to start you off:

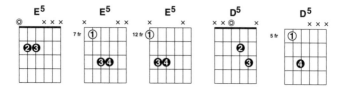

Power Fourths

If you turn a fifth upside-down you get a fourth: CG becomes GC. Fourths are another useful trick when playing rock guitar. They don't work as well for chugging rhythm figures but they do make great riffs and can also feature in lead guitar solos.

Here are some examples.

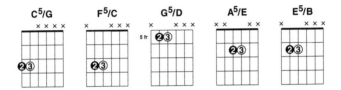

You may find it easier to play these using a first-finger barre. Try the examples below:

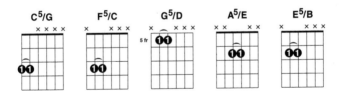

Although these chords are called 4ths we write them as slash chords to avoid confusing them with another type of chord called a 'sus4'. C5/G just means a C power-chord with the G at the bottom.

Perfect Barre Chords

One of the more difficult techniques for guitar is the barre chord. A barre chord involves holding more than one string down with the same finger - often the first, but sometimes the third or fourth.

To start with, most players find it hard holding down more than one string with the same finger. You will need to build some strength in your fretting hand, but here are some other quick-fix solutions:

String Action

Make sure that the action (the height of the strings above the fretboard) on your guitar is low. This will instantly help you hold down more strings. If it is too high, take it into a guitar shop to have it adjusted.

Lighter Strings

Try moving to a lighter string gauge. Lighter strings need less tension and are therefore easier to press down.

Thumb Position

Make sure that your fretting hand's thumb remains vertical but drops below the neck to enable the fingers to open out and stretch. If you are not using your second finger in the chord try putting it on top of the first finger making the barre in order to increase the pressure.

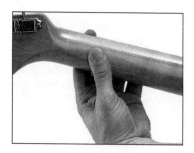

Barre Technique

When you barre with your first finger, roll the finger very slightly toward the headstock end of the neck. By exerting more pressure with that edge of the finger you can make a better contact.

Don't practise barre chords always at the first fret. String tension is usually high there because the string is right next to the nut. Try moving a few frets up.

These chords will help you gradually develop your barre. Try playing them at higher frets until you have built up strength in your fretting hand. Then move them back down to the bottom of the neck.

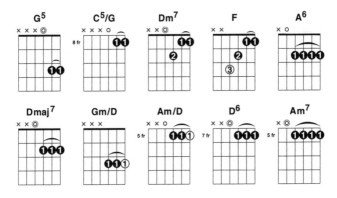

Single String Altered Tuning (1)

Experimenting with altered tunings can be a little confusing. If you change as few as three or four strings the layout of notes on the fretboard can become unrecognisable. This can make you feel lost! Fortunately you don't have to go that far.

Start by changing one string and experimenting with the new chords you discover.

We've seen what happens when you take the bottom string - E - down to D. So why not do the reverse and take the top E down to D instead? To check the new tuning, either compare the top string with the fourth (D) or compare it with the D that's at the third fret on the B string.

Here are some chords from that tuning. Notice that boxes 6-10 contain familiar shapes that now sound different because of just one string being changed.

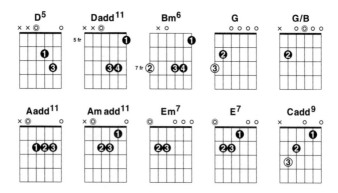

Single String Altered Tuning (2)

Here's another tuning that only needs a single string alteration. Take the third string G down a semitone to F♯. You can use the F♯ that's at the fourth fret on the D string as a reference point.

As before, some familiar shapes now sound different and there are some new shapes. Notice in particular the beautifully resonant B / Bm chords which in standard tuning would be barre chords but here are full of open strings!

Tuning Guide						
String number	6	5	4	3	2	1
Standard tuning	E	A	D	G	B	E
This tuning	E	A	D	F♯	B	E
Alteration necessary	-	-	-	-1	-	-
Interval between strings (in semitones/frets)	5	5	4	5	5	

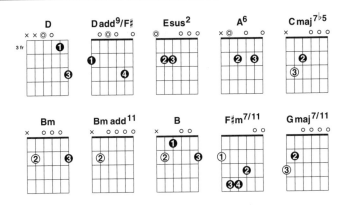

A Classic Rock'n'Roll Rhythm Figure (1)

Here's a famous rock'n'roll rhythm figure, used since the 1950s.

In the first bar you'll see the E5 / E6 riff played low down. Try to strike both notes evenly. This also works if you move it up to the A string and D string.

In the second bar the riff is played one octave higher. Keep your thumb behind the neck so that your fingers can stretch to finger these notes. In the third bar the figure is played at the same pitch but one string higher at the 7th fret.

Bars 2 and 3 are moveable patterns (i.e. they don't use any open strings) so you can use these riff patterns for any chord.

If you were playing a 12-bar in the key of A you could start on the bottom string at fret 5 and play the D and E chords on the 5th string at frets 5 and 7. Alternatively you could start on the 5th string at fret 12 and then move down from there. Try to memorise the shape of these movements.

A Classic Rock'n'Roll Rhythm Figure (2)

This full-blooded rhythm lick makes a great complement to the one on the facing page. Using more notes, it has a fatter sound.

It works like this: play an A chord at the second fret using a first finger barre. This is the position for an A6 chord but you're not going to hit the top string, just the middle four. Your third finger adds a note on the D string and then takes it off - just as you did with the previous example.

To play this on other chords is slightly more tricky. For example, when the riff is moved up to B, the bass note can only be fingered by the little finger reaching onto the bottom string and deadening the 5th at the same time. This requires practice. If you find it too difficult, just leave the bass note out and turn the figure into three notes only.

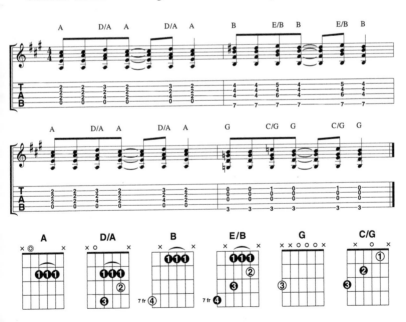

A Little Bit Of Eastern Promise

There are three main types of minor scale: the natural, the harmonic and the melodic. Of these, the harmonic is the most unusual in sound. This is because it has a gap of three semitones between the 6th and 7th notes with a semitone before and after.

It is easy to take this part of the scale and exploit it for an 'Eastern' sounding lead line, as this example shows. It sounds even more exotic with the addition of string bends, in the third and fourth bars.

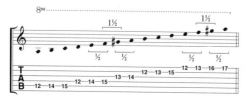

A Harmonic Minor

Watch the stretches between the 6th and 7th notes of the scale; it's this interval that is responsible for the scale's unusual sound. Check out the solo in *Don't Fear The Reaper* by Blue Oyster Cult to hear the Harmonic Minor Scale in action!

Alternate Picking For Indie Guitar

So-called 'indie' guitar styles are often chordally-based and involve playing chord arpeggios. Sometimes this involves rapid picking of the strings. To do that successfully it is important to practise alternate picking.

Alternate picking means playing down and up strokes with the pick, thus making the most use of each pick movement. If you've picked a note downward why not hit it again coming back up, instead of coming back up just for the next down stroke?

Try the following chord sequence with strict alternate picking: down up down up etc. Start off slowly and then gradually speed it up, aiming for a steady sound, and not looking at the strings.

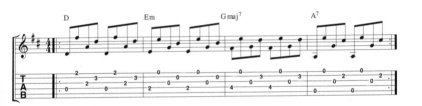

For a typical indie sound, you could try playing this on a 12-string Rickenbacker, but you can create an approximation by adding a small amount of chorus and reverb to any electric guitar. Check out the recordings of Johnny Marr (The Smiths), Peter Buck (R.E.M.) and John Squire (Stone Roses) to hear this style in action.

Better Tone For Fingerstyle Guitar

Here's a neat tip for fingerstyle players who like to use their nails. Have you noticed how your picking fingers can catch on the strings, causing you to stumble over some passages?

To help reduce the friction of the nail against the string, get some very fine emery paper. Use it to round off any hard edges so that your nail has a smooth curve from one side to the other.

Then use the paper to bevel the inside edge of the nail (between the nail and the finger). You can achieve this by holding the edge of the nail at an angle to the paper. This puts a slight slope on the inside edge of the nail. When the string hits this it will slide off.

The result: less of a feeling that your fingers are catching against the strings and a better tone.

Hendrix-Style Rhythm (1)

The legendary playing of Jimi Hendrix has many facets. Although people often think of him tearing lead lick after lead lick from an amped-up Stratocaster, he was also an innovative rhythm player.

Here's a Hendrix-type rhythm lick to introduce a song or support a verse. Imagine playing this and singing at the same time! Although each bar clearly implies the chords, you can also think of these phrases as based on the pentatonic major scale. Notice how the slides add to the fluid feel and how the same fingering can be used on either the bottom string or the fifth.

In the right musical context this can be an interesting alternative to just strumming the chords.

Hendrix-Style Rhythm (2)

This next example is based on Hendrix's much-admired use of what is known as a 'broken-chord' accompaniment. It sounds complicated when you hear it, but once you grasp the basic idea behind the approach it is much easier. Gene's Steve Mason is another guitarist who uses it.

The trick to playing 'broken-chord' accompaniments is to find a barre chord which can be held down with one finger leaving the others free. This often means playing only a triad – in other words three or four strings which give you the essential notes. Playing two adjacent strings at a time you then use a finger to hammer-on and/or pull-off notes that don't belong in the chord. This produces tension-and-release patterns which can be very expressive.

Triad Chords

Here are some examples. Using a fifth finger barre, use the third finger to hammer on successive strings to produce a rising/ falling pattern. Try pulling-off as well.

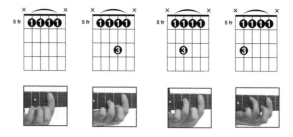

It is also possible to reverse this. Using slightly different finger-ings the extra note(s) end up under the barre so that the hammer-on actually completes the chord and removes the tension.

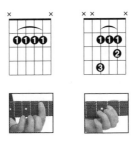

This example gives you a taste of this technique. Try to relate what you're playing to the implied barre chord shape in each instance. Play very slowly – this suits a gentle ballad.

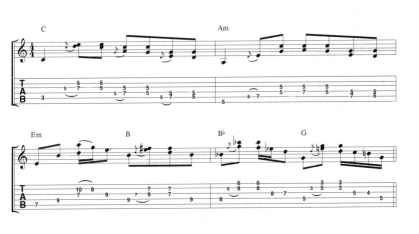

How To Start A Blues Solo

Here's a classic set of blues lead licks for the first four bars of a 12-bar in A.

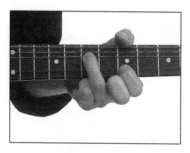

Unison Bends

Check out the unison bend effect which happens in every bar - D is bent to E and then an E is hit straight after it. Hold the top two notes down with your first finger as a half-barre and use your third finger to bend the string.

These phrases can be played in any order and in any key - just move them up or down the fretboard as required.

The root note is on the top string at the 5th fret in the first bar (A) so if you wanted to play these phrases in C you would move that note to the 8th fret and play the same fingerings at that position.

Knopfler-Style Rhythm

Most of the unique guitar sound on Dire Straits' "Sultans of Swing" album came from Mark Knopfler's distinctive picking style. Using a thumb and two fingers to pluck the strings, and resting the third and little fingers on the guitar body, makes it natural to play triads which only use three strings.

Try this technique with the example below.

You'll find that playing with your fingers, rather than a pick, opens up many more possibilities of tone and articulation. Experiment with striking the strings with your fingertips, or try catching a little bit of nail as you pick. Similarly, where you pick the string can change the sound considerably - listen to the change in sound as you pick near the bridge, or right up by the fingerboard.

More Blues Licks

The greatest amount of chord movement in a 12-bar occurs in the last four bars (9-12) - this is called the 'turnaround' because it leads from the end of one 12-bar sequence back into the beginning of another. Here's a neat phrase that you can just move around as the chords change.

Notice the E at fret 9 in bar 1. That's the root note of the chord over which you're playing. Use that note to locate the phrase somewhere else on the neck if you want to play in a different key.

A 12-bar in G would have a D chord in bar 9, so you would locate that note at fret 7. In fact, this is what happens in bar 2 of this example: everything would move down two frets.

Tip For A Quick-Change Blues

In blues there is a form known as the 'quick-change' 12-bar. Instead of having four bars of the key chord with the first change coming in bar 5:

A 'quick-change' blues changes chord in bar 2 and then returns to the key chord in bar 3:

The following simple trick enables you to exploit this when soloing. If you play the first bar on the A pentatonic minor scale at the 5th fret simply move the pattern up two frets in bar 2. You will be on a D pentatonic major scale, which will make a pleasing and highly professional-sounding contrast for that bar, instead of staying with the more predictable A pentatonic minor. The same two frets up trick will work in any other bar where there is a D: i.e. in bars 5-6 and 10.

Writing Songs

Many guitarists would like to write songs but don't necessarily know which chords go together. There is a simple formula for working this out. Let's pick a guitar friendly key: C major.

The notes of C major are: C D E F G A B C. They are separated by a pattern of intervals: tone, tone semitone, tone, tone, tone, semitone (in frets 2 2 1 2 2 2 1). The chords of C major are formed from these notes and follow a fixed sequence: major, minor, minor, major, major, minor, diminished.

Therefore, the chords that sound good together in C major are C Dm Em F G and Am. The seventh chord, B diminished, can be ignored as it is not often used. We get an acceptable substitute by flattening the seventh note from B to B♭ and turning it into a B♭ major. Here are the chords formed from the scale:

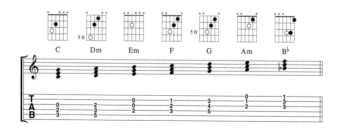

Here are the same chords for other guitar-friendly keys:

F major:

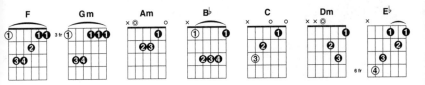

G major:

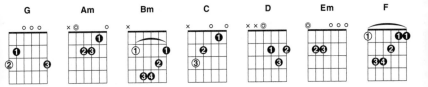

D major:

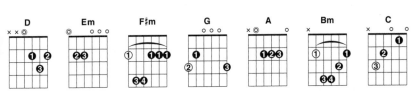

Choose any key and you are free to combine the seven chords in any way you like. Many famous songs use only three or four of the seven!

04/07 (62024)

Check out some of these other books to expand your guitar-playing potential!

The Wah Wah Book
History, technique, perspectives, philosophy, product info- everything you need to know about the Wah Wah pedal.
AM931580

Riff Tricks
Listen to the tape and follow the guitar tab to create your own rock, pop and blues guitar riffs. You'll be playing like a pro in no time!
AM83163

300 Tips and Tricks for Guitar
A practical guide for every guitarist. Includes hints on reading music, playing chords, scales and riffs and blues, rock and country styles.
AM945220

Practical Pentatonics
An introduction to pentatonic patterns, theory and usage. Dozens of creative examples, plus valuable tips on developing your own pentatonic licks.
AM68123

The Advanced Guitar Case Chord Book
A concise thesaurus of essential and practical advanced guitar chord forms for study and practice. Includes valuable tips on chord and music theory and musical examples.
AM80227